Answer the questions.

1.
a bus

Is it an airplane?
No, it is not an airplane.
It is a bus.

2.
a door

Is it a doll?
No, it is not __ _____.
It is __ _____.

3.
a teacher

Is he a police officer?
No, he ___ ____ ___ _____ _____.
___ ___ ___ _____.

4.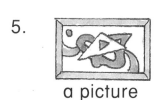
a hand

Is it a foot?
No, ___ ___ ___ ___ _____.
___ ___ ___ _____.

5.
a picture

Is it a wheel?
___, ___ ___ ___ ___ _____.
___ ___ ___ _____.

6.
a police officer

Is he a bus driver?
___, ___ ___ ___ ___ ___ ___ _____.
___ ___ ___ _____ _____.

7.
a shirt

Is it a newspaper?
___, ___ ___ ___ ___ _____.
___ ___ ___ _____.

Review

Write the questions and answers.

1.

Where is the car?
It is under the tree.

2.

Where is the boat?
It is on the table.

3.

Where ___ the ball?
It ___ in the river.

4.

Where ___ ___ lamp?
___ is ___ ___ table.

5.

_____ is the spoon?
___ ___ in ___ bowl.

6.

_____ ___ ___ cat?
It ___ in ___ box.

7.

_____ ___ ___ flower?
___ ___ in ___ cup.

8.

_____ ___ ___ bus?
___ ___ under ___ table.

2

Finish the sentences.

1. four glasses

   There are four glasses on the table.

2. two cats

   There are ____ _____ on the roof.

3. eight pencils

   There ____ _____ _____ on the table.

4. two clocks

   _____ are ____ _____ on ____ desk.

5. three shoes

   _____ ____ _____ _____ under ____ chair.

6. six oranges

   _____ ___ ____ _____ ___ ____ basket.

7. seven bottles

   _____ ___ ____ _____ ___ ____ cupboard.

8. nine matches

   _____ ___ ____ _____ ___ ____ box.

Review

Answer the questions.

1.
running

What is John doing?
He is running.
  What are the children doing?
  They are _____ ___ ____ box.

2.
standing on

3.
holding
a book

What is Mary doing?
____ ___ _____ __ ____.
  What are the men doing?
  They ____ _____ __ ____.

4.
pushing
a car

5.
carrying
a basket

What is the woman doing?
____ ___ _____ __ _____.
  What is Peter doing?
  ___ __ _____ __ __ ___.

6.
sitting on
a wall

7.
drawing
on the
blackboard

What are the girls doing?
____ ___ _____ ___ ___
_____.
  What is Mr. Lee doing?
  __ __ _____ __ ___.

8.
driving
a car

9.
reading
a book

What are you doing?
I ___ _____ __ ____.
  What are you doing?
  __ __ _____ ___ ___.

10.
sitting on a
chair

4

Review

John   Peter   Tom   Mary   Ann   Mimi

Answer the questions.

1. Who has a white shirt? John does.
   He has a white shirt.

2. Who has a black dress? Mary and Ann do.
   They have black dresses.

3. Who has a black shirt? _____

   _____ .

4. Who has a white dress? _____

   _____ .

5. Who has white pants? _____

   _____ .

6. Who has black pants? _____

   _____ .

7. Who has black shoes? All the boys do.

   _____ .

8. Who has white shoes? _____

   _____ .

5

Answer the questions.

1. What is your name?

   ___ _____ is _____.

2. What is your teacher's name?

   ___ _____ name ___ _____.

3. Is there a book on your desk?

   _____, _____ ___.

4. Is there a teacher in the room?

   _____, _____ ___.

5. Are there children in the room?

   _____, _____ _____.

6. Are there cats and dogs in the room?

   _____, _____ ____ _____.

7. How many boys are there in your class?

   _____ ____ _____.

8. Where is the teacher's desk?

   _____.

9. What is on the wall?

   _____.

10. Where are you sitting?

    _____.

11. What color is the board?

    _____.

12. What are you doing now?

    _____.

a piece

chalk

This is a piece of chalk.

a glass

milk

This ___ __ __ _____ __ _____ .

a piece

string

___ __ __ _____ __ _____ .

a bottle

ink

___ __ __ _____ __ _____ .

a bowl

soup

___ __ __ _____ __ _____ .

a piece

paper

___ __ __ _____ __ _____ .

a cup

tea

___ __ __ _____ __ _____ .

Write.

1. I can see. I ____ hear. __ ____ speak.

2. I can ___ the board.

3. The teacher is not talking. I ____ see the teacher but I cannot ____ the teacher.

4. I ____ write with a pen but I _____ write with an umbrella.

5. I ____ see the ceiling but I _____ _____ an airplane.

6. Can you see an eraser?   Thank _____.
   Now I can clean _____ _____.

7. Can you see a marker?   _____ you.
   Now I _____ write on _____ _____.

Write questions and answers.

1.

Can you see the bowl of soup?

Yes, I can. I like soup.

2.

Can you see the piece ___ chicken?

Yes, __ ____ . I _____ chicken.

3.

Can ____ _____ __ _____ of milk?

Yes, ____ ____ . I _____ _____ .

4.

Can ____ ___ __ ____ ___ tea?

Yes, __ ___ . __ ___ ___ .

5.

_____ of fish?

_____ .

6.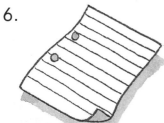

_____ piece _____ ?

_____ .

Finish the sentences.

1. thick

This book is thick
    but this book is thin.

thin

2. open

This door is open
_____ this door is _____.

shut

3. happy

This girl is happy
_____ _____ girl ___ _____.

unhappy

4. tall

This woman is tall
___ ___ ___ ___ ___ ___.

short

5. big

This dog is big
_____.

small

6. clean

This boy is clean
_____.

dirty

7. abcd efgh
good

This writing is good
_____.

abcd efgh
bad

8. white

This cat is white
_____.

black

Finish the sentences.

1. a bag

This is a bag.

2. a box

That is __ ____.

3. a picture

That _____.

4. a book

This _____.

5. a tree

_____.

6. a flower

_____.

7. an airplane

_____.

8. a bird

_____.

Finish the sentences.

1. These are glasses but those _____ bottles.

2. These _____ oranges but those _____ apples.

3. _____ _____ socks but _____ _____ shoes.

4. _____ _____ girls _____ _____ _____ boys.

5. _____

   _____ .

1. Is this a bell or a hammer?
It is not a bell.
It is a hammer.

2. Is this a circle or a square?
It ___ not a _____.
___ ___ ___ _____.

3. Is this a car or a truck?
___ ___ not ___ _____.
___ ___ ___ _____.

4. Is this a pen or a pencil?
_____.
_____.

5. Is this a collar or a tie?
_____.
_____.

6. Is this the back of the car or the front?
_____.
_____.

7. Is this coffee or milk?
_____.
_____.

13

1.

Are these cats or dogs?
They are not cats.
They are dogs.

2.

Are these fingers or needles?
They ____ not _____.
_____ ____ _____.

3.

Are these buttons or apples?
_____ ____ not _____.
_____.

4.

Are these cups or glasses?
_____.
_____.

5.

Are these eggs or bottles?
_____.
_____.

6.

Are these tables or desks?
_____.
_____.

7.

Are these eyes or lips?
_____.
_____.

Finish the sentences.

1. Are these buses or cars?

 This is a bus but that  is a car.

2. Are these cats or dogs?

 These are cats but those  are dogs.

3. Are these bells or drums?

 _____ is a _____ but that is __ _____.

4. Are these cups ___ glasses?

 _____ are _____ but _____  are _____.

5. ____ these pieces of chicken ___ pieces ___ fish?

  that
_____.

6. ____ _____ pins or nails?

 _____
_____.

Write **Please** *or* **Please don't**.

1. _____ listen to me.

2. _____ run across the street.

3. _____ fight.

4. _____ walk on the path.

5. _____ write on the wall.

6. _____ sit on the chair.

7. _____ run in the school.

8. _____ walk on the sidewalk.

9. _____ stand up.

10. _____ talk.

A. *Put a circle around the right word.*

   1. I am touching she/her/he.

   2. We are listening to he/him/we.

   3. She is carrying it/he/I.

   4. He is helping we/they/us.

   5. He is sitting near I/we/me.

   6. She is talking to they/them/we.

   7. She is pointing to you/they/we.

   8. They are looking at we/us/I.

B. *Write* **me**, **you**, **him**, **her**, **it**, **us**, *or* **them**.

   1. I want the apple. Please give it to _____.

   2. Listen to Miss Lee. She is talking to _____.

   3. This is John. I am touching _____.

   4. This is Mary. I am touching _____.

   5. Please sit on the chair. Don't stand on _____.

   6. We are listening to the teacher. She is telling _____ a story.

   7. John and Peter are working and I am helping _____.

   8. Mary has a kitten. She is carrying _____.

   9. We are listening to the teacher. She is talking to _____.

   10. Please listen to me. I am talking to _____.

   11. Peter is my friend. I am sitting near _____.

   12. Mary is my friend. I am sitting near _____.

Finish the sentences.

1.

You are standing on the chair.

Don't stand on it.

2.

You are standing on the desk.

Don't _____ ___ ___.

3.

You are eating the cookies.

_____ ____ them.

4.

You are breaking the glasses.

_____.

5.

You are pushing that girl.

_____.

6.

You are laughing at me.

_____.

Finish the sentences.

1. John is running. Peter is running.

   John is running and Peter is running, too.

2. Mary is walking. Ann is walking.

   Mary is walking _____ Ann is walking, too.

3. The men are smiling. The women are smiling.

   The men are smiling ____ ____ _____ ____ _____, ____.

4. The boys are drinking. The girls are drinking.

   The boys ____ _____ ____ ____ _____ ____ _____,

   ____.

5. Peter's shirt is yellow. John's shirt is yellow.

   Peter's _____ John's

   _____.

6. Mary's shoes are white. Ann's shoes are white.

   _____.

7. The teacher is drawing a flower. The children are drawing a

   flower. _____.

8. The teacher's dress is blue. Mary's dress is blue.

   _____

   _____.

9. Mr. Lee's car is red. Mr. Hall's car is red.

   _____

   _____.

10. Mary's writing is good. Ann's writing is good.

    _____.

Finish the sentences.

1. John has a pen. Peter has a pen.

   John has a pen and Peter has one, too.

2. Mary has a book. Ann has a book.

   Mary has a book and _____ _____ one, too.

3. Mr. Lee has a car. Mr. Hall has a car.

   Mr. Lee _____ __ _____ and Mr. Hall _____ _____, _____.

4. Mrs. Hall has a basket. Mrs. Lee has a basket.

   Mrs. Hall _____.

5. Peter is holding a book. John is holding a book.

   Peter _____

   _____.

6. Ann is holding a basket. Mary is holding a basket.

   Ann _____

   _____.

7. Peter is wearing shoes. John is wearing shoes.

   Peter _____

   _____.

8. The men are wearing hats. The women are wearing hats.

   The men _____

   _____.

9. I have a pencil. John has a pencil.

   _____.

10. We have a picture. They have a picture.

   _____

   _____.

Finish the sentences.

1.

The man is old.
He is an ____ man.
He is not a young ____.

2.

The dog is dirty.
It is a _____ ____.
It is not a clean ____.

3.

The woman is unhappy.
She is an _____ _____.
She __ __ __ _____
_____.

4.

The dog is little.
It ___ ___ _____ dog.
___ ___ not __ ____ ____.

5.

The flag is long.
It ___ __ ____ ____.
___ ___ ____ __ short ____.

21

Finish the sentences.

1.

big
little

The big dog is behind the tree.

The _____ dog is in front of the tree.

2.

old
young

The old man is on the chair.

____ _____ man is behind the chair.

3.

black
white

The black cat is on the table.

__ _____ _____ ___ under the table.

4.

short
long

The short ruler is on the book.

____ _____ _____ ___ in ____ _____ .

5.

thin
fat

The thin boy is in front of the tree.

___ ___ ___ ___ _____ _____
_____ .

6.

big
little

The big dog is next to the basket.

___ _____ ___ __ _____
_____ .

7.

clean
dirty

The clean shirt is on the table.

__ _____ _____ __ __ ____ floor.

8.

unhappy
happy

The unhappy boy is in the water.

___ ____ ___ __ __ ____ boat.

22

Color the pictures. Write **Our**, **Your**, **Their**, **Its**.

1. We have red books. Our books are red.

2. You have green books. _____ books are green.

3. They have red hats.  _____ hats are red.

4. The car has red wheels.  _____ wheels are red.

5. We have blue shoes.  _____ shoes are blue.

6. You have green shoes.  _____ shoes are green.

7. They have yellow rulers.  _____ rulers are yellow.

8. The cat has a black tail.  _____ tail is black.

9. We have red pens.  _____ pens are red.

Finish the sentences.

1. Is his hair short or long?
    His hair is short. He has short hair.

2. Is his hair short or long?
    _____ hair is _____. He has _____ _____.

3. Is her dress short or long?
    Her _____.
    She has a _____.

4. Is its tail long or short?
    Its _____.
    It _____.

5. Is its tail long or short?
    _____.
    It _____.

6. Are their hats white or black?
    Their _____.
    They _____.

7. Are their shoes black or white?
    _____.
    _____.

8. Is your school big or small?
    Our _____.
    We _____.

24

Finish the sentences.

1. Does he have any rulers? Does he have any pens?
He has some rulers but he doesn't have any pens.

2. Does she have any apples? Does she have any oranges?
She has _____ apples but she doesn't have _____ oranges.

3. Does he have any books? Does he have any rulers?
He _____ _____ _____ but __ _____ _____
_____ _____.

4. Does she have any rulers? Does she have any pencils?
She _____
_____.

5. Does she have any flowers? Does she have any oranges?
_____
_____.

6. Does it have _____ legs? Does it have _____ arms?
_____
_____.

7. _____ he _____ __ bottles? _____ __ _____
_____ cups? _____
_____.

8. _____ __ _____ _____ shoes? _____ __ _____ _____
socks? _____
_____.

Finish the sentences.

1.
no legs

This doll doesn't have any legs.
It has no legs.

2.
no legs

This chair _____ _____ ____ _____.
It ____ no _____.

3.
no wheels

This car _____ _____ ____ _____.
It ____ ___ _____.

4.
no hair

This man _____ _____ ____ _____.
He _____.

5.
no tails

These cats don't have ____ _____.
_____.

6.
no collars

These dogs _____ ____ ____ _____.
_____.

7.
no shoes

These _____ _____ ____ _____.
_____.

8.
no shirts

These _____ _____ ____ _____.
_____.

Finish the sentences.

The man has a lot of books.

The woman doesn't have many _____.

The girl doesn't have any _____.

The boy _____ _____ _____ books.

The man has __ _____ of glasses.

The woman _____ _____ _____ glasses.

The girl _____ _____ any _____.

The boy _____ _____ _____ _____.

The woman _____ __ _____ _____ cups.

The man _____ _____ _____ _____.

The girl _____ _____ _____ _____.

The boy _____ _____ _____ _____.

Write sentences.

1. apples/oranges

   Mrs. Lowe has a lot of apples but she doesn't have many oranges.

2. ties/socks

   Mr. Hall has __ _____ ____ ties but he doesn't have _____ socks.

3. brothers/sisters

   This boy _____ __ _____ ____ brothers ____ he _____ _____ many _____ .

4. pears/bananas

   Mary _____ but she doesn't have _____ .

5. plates/cookies

   Peter _____ _____ .

6. trees/flowers

   The garden has _____ but it _____ .

7. flags/sailors

   The ship _____ it doesn't have _____ .

8. windows/doors

   The room _____ _____ .

1.

Is there any milk? Is there any ink?
There is some milk but there isn't any ink.

2.

Is there any ink? Is there any milk?
There is _____ _____ but there _____ _____
_____ .

3.

Is there any chalk? Is there any bread?
_____
but _____ .

4.

Is there any rice? Is there any chalk?
_____
_____ .

5.

Is there any bread? Is there any chalk?
_____
_____ .

6.

Is there any water? Is there any milk?
_____
_____ .

7.

Is there any tea? Is there any ink?
_____
_____ .

8.

Is there any ice? Is there any milk?
_____
_____ .

1. How much milk is there?

There is a lot of milk.

There _____ much milk.

There _____ any milk.

2. How much ink is there?

There is ___ _____ ____ ink.

There isn't _____ _____.

There _____ _____ _____.

3. How much sand is there?

There _____.

_____.

_____.

4. How much smoke is there?

_____.

_____.

_____.

Answer the questions.

1. Are there any desks in your classroom?

   Yes, there are. There are some desks.

2. Are there any windows in your classroom?

   Yes, _____ _____. There are _____ _____.

3. Are there any horses in your classroom?

   No, there aren't. There _____ any _____.

4. Are there any children in your classroom?

   Yes, _____ _____. There _____ _____ _____.

5. Are there any dogs in your classroom?

   No, _____ _____. _____ _____ _____ _____.

6. Are there any pictures in your classroom?

   Yes, _____ _____. _____ _____ _____ _____.

7. Are there any boys in your classroom?

   _____, _____. _____.

8. Are there any girls in your classroom?

   _____, _____. _____.

9. Are there any cats in your classroom?

   No, _____.

10. Are there any books in your classroom?

    _____.

31

Write the questions and the answers.

1. books   Are there any books on the table?

   Yes, _____ ____. There ____ _____ _____.

2. shoes   ____ there any shoes on the table?

   No, _____ aren't. There _____ ____ _____.

3. boxes   ____ _____ any boxes on the table?

   Yes, _____ ____. _____ ____ _____ _____.

4. cats   ____ _____ ____ cats on the table?

   No, _____ _____. _____ ____ ___ ____.

5. apples   _____ ____ ___ apples ___ ____ _____?

   ____, _____ ____ ____. _____ ____ ____ ____ _____.

6. chairs   _____?

   _____ . _____ .

7. cups   _____?

   _____ . _____ .

8. glasses   _____?

   _____ . _____ .

count - are ___s
many
non count - ___is
much

1. glasses   milk
2. rice   plates
3. crackers   bread
4. water   cups
5. cookies   coffee
6. paper   pencils
7. pens   ink
8. sugar   candy

Finish the sentences.

1. There are a lot of glasses in the cupboard but there isn't much milk.

2. There is ___ _____ ____ rice in the cupboard but there aren't _____ plates.

3. There are ___ _____ ____ crackers ____ _____ _____ but there ____ much bread.

4. There is _____ but there aren't _____.

5. There _____ but _____.

6. _____ _____.

7. _____ _____.

8. _____ _____.

1. bus   2. bus   3. foot

4. car   5. boat   6. plane

Look at the pictures and answer the questions.

1. How is the boy going to school?
   He is going to school by bus.

2. How is the girl going to school?

   _____.

3. How are they going to school?

   _____.

4. How is the man going to work?

   _____.

5. How are they crossing the river?

   _____.

6. How are they going to Chicago?

   _____.

7. How do **you** go to school?

   I _____.

Answer the questions.

1.　　　　　glass

milk

What is the glass made of?
It is made of glass.
What is it full of?
It is full of milk.

2.　　　　　glass

ink

What is the bottle made of?
It ____ _____ ____ glass.
What is it full of?
It ____ _____ ____ ink.

3.　　　　　tin

coffee

What is the can made of?

_____.

What is it full of?

_____.

4.　　　　　wood

chalk

What is the box made of?

_____.

What is it full of?

_____.

35

Review

Answer the questions.

1.

John is going to
school.

What is it time for?
It is time for school.
What is John carrying?
He is carrying a bag.
What is the bag full of?
It is full of books.

2.

Mary is going to
school.

What is it time for?
It is _____.
What is Mary carrying?
She _____.
What is it full of?

_____.

3.

Mr. Rose is going to
work.

What is it time for?

_____.
What is Mr. Rose riding on?

_____.
What is the bus full of?
_____ people.

4.

Ann is having lunch.

What is it time for?

_____.
What is Ann holding?

_____.
What is the glass full of?

_____.

| May I | open
close | the door,
the window, | please? |
| | have
take | a cookie,
a new book, | |

Write eight questions and answers.

1. May I open the door, _____? Yes, you may.

2. _____ __ close the door, _____? Yes, _____ _____.

3. _____ __ open _____ _____, _____? _____, _____ _____.

4. _____?

_____.

5. _____?

_____.

6. _____?

_____.

7. _____?

_____.

8. _____?

_____.

What are they?

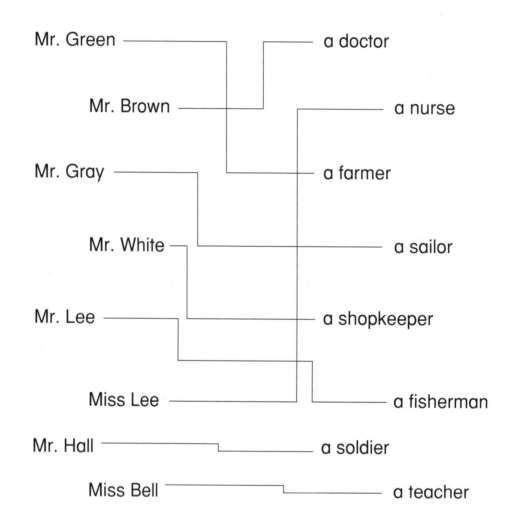

Mr. Green	a doctor
Mr. Brown	a nurse
Mr. Gray	a farmer
Mr. White	a sailor
Mr. Lee	a shopkeeper
Miss Lee	a fisherman
Mr. Hall	a soldier
Miss Bell	a teacher

1. Mr. Green is a farmer.

2. Mr. Brown _____.

3. _____.

4. _____.

5. _____.

6. _____.

7. _____.

8. _____.

Review

1.

a firefighter?

Is he a firefighter?
No, he isn't. He is a laborer.

2.

a gardener?

Is he a gardener?
No, _____ .
He _____ .

3.

a baker?

Is she a _____ ?
No, _____ .
_____ .

4.

a doctor?

Is _____ ?
_____ .
_____ .

5.

a soldier?

_____ ?
_____ .
_____ .

6.

a teacher?

_____ ?
_____ .
_____ .

39

old—older   short—shorter
tall—taller   fast—faster
small—smaller   slow—slower
young—younger   strong—stronger

big—bigger
thin—thinner
fat—fatter

Write in the words.

1. A man is older than a boy.   (old)
2. A tree is _____ _____ a flower.   (tall)
3. A cat is _____ _____ a dog.   (small)
4. A girl is _____ _____ a woman.   (young)
5. A pencil is _____ _____ a ruler.   (short)
6. An airplane is _____ _____ a car.   (fast)
7. A bicycle is _____ _____ a car.   (slow)
8. A man is _____ _____ a boy.   (strong)
9. A horse is _____ _____ a dog.   (big)
10. A newspaper is _____ _____ a book.   (thin)
11. A duck is _____ _____ a hen.   (fat)

happy—happier   beautiful—more beautiful
greedy—greedier   clever—cleverer
heavy—heavier   careless—more careless
easy—easier

Finish the sentences.

1. This girl is happy
   but this girl is _____ .

2. This boy is greedy
   but this _____ ____ _____ .

3. This box is heavy
   but _____ ____ ____ _____ .

4. This is easy
   ____ _____ ____ _____ .

5. This picture is beautiful _____
   _____ .

6. This boy is clever _____
   _____ .

7. This work is careless _____
   _____ .

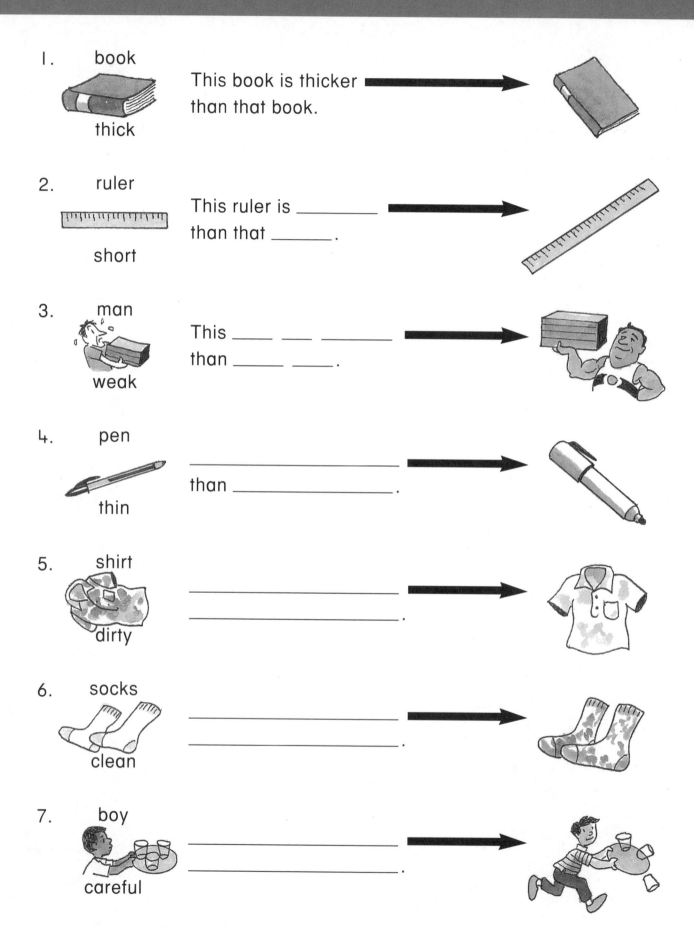

1. book

   thick

   This book is thicker than that book. ➡

2. ruler

   short

   This ruler is _____ than that _____. ➡

3. man

   weak

   This ____ __ _____ than _____ ____. ➡

4. pen

   thin

   _____ than _____. ➡

5. shirt

   dirty

   _____ _____. ➡

6. socks

   clean

   _____ _____. ➡

7. boy

   careful

   _____ _____. ➡

42

Finish the sentences.

1. Where is my umbrella?
Here is your umbrella.
Here it is!

2. Where are my books?
_____ are your books.
_____ they are!

3. Where is my hat?
_____ _____ your hat.
_____ _____ is!

4. Where are my shoes?
_____ _____ _____ shoes.
_____ _____ ____!

5. Where is my shirt?
_____ _____ _____ shirt.
_____ ____ ____!

6. Where are my apples?
_____ _____ _____ apples.
_____ ____ ____!

7. Where is my bag?
_____ _____ _____ bag.
_____ ____ ____!

Finish the sentences.

1. Where are the children?
There are the children.
There _____ are!

2. Where is the kite?
There _____ the kite.
There _____ _____!

3. Where are my glasses?
_____ _____ your glasses.
_____ _____ _____!

4. Where is the fire?
_____ _____ _____ fire.
_____ _____ _____!

5. Where is our boat?
_____ _____ your _____.
_____ _____ _____!

6. Where are my cats?
_____ _____ _____ cats.
_____ _____ _____!

7. Where is the bus?
_____ _____ _____ _____.
_____ _____ _____!

Write **anything, something,** *or* **nothing.**

1.

Is there anything in the bottle?
Yes, there is. There is _____ in the bottle.

2.

Is there anything in the bottle?
No, there isn't. There isn't anything in the bottle.
There is _____ in the bottle.

3.

Is there _____ in the glass?
Yes, there is. There is _____ in the glass.

4.

Is there _____ in the glass?
No, there isn't. There isn't _____ in the glass.
There is _____ in the glass.

5.

Is there _____ in the box?
No, there isn't. There isn't _____ in the box.
There is _____ in the box.

6.

Is there _____ in the cupboard?
No, there isn't. There isn't _____ in the
cupboard. There is _____ in the cupboard.

7.

Is there _____ on the board?
Yes, there is. There is _____ on the board.

Write **anyone, someone,** *or* **no one.**

1.

Is there anyone in the car?
Yes, there is. There is _____ in the car.

2.

Is there _____ in the car?
No, there isn't. There isn't _____ in the car.
There is _____ in the car.

3.

Is there _____ on the bus?
Yes, there is. There is _____ on the bus.

4.

Is there _____ on the bus?
No, there isn't. There isn't _____ on the bus.
There is _____ on the bus.

5.

Is there anyone in the classroom? No, there isn't.
There isn't _____ in the classroom.
There is _____ in the classroom.

6.

Is there _____ in the classroom?
Yes, there is. There is _____ in the classroom.

7.

Is there _____ on the train?
No, there isn't. There isn't _____ on the train.
There is _____ on the train.

Write the questions and answers.

1.
_____ there anything on the table?
Yes, _____ is. There ____ something ____
____ _____ .

2.
__ _____ _____ __ ___ _____?
No, _____ ____ . There ___ anything on the
table. There ___ nothing __ ___ _____ .

3.
__ _____ _____ ___ _____ chair?
Yes, _____ ____ . There ____ _____
____ _____ chair.

4.
__ _____ _____ __ ___ _____?
No, _____ _____ . There isn't _____
__ ___ chair. _____ is _____ __ __
_____ .

5.
Is _____ _____ __ ____ cupboard?
__ , _____ _____ . There isn't _____
__ ___ _____ . There __ _____
__ ___ _____ .

47

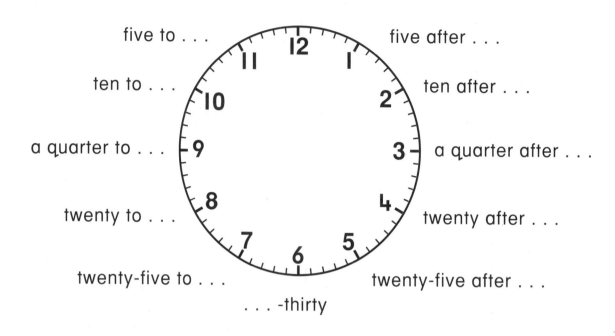

five to . . .

ten to . . .

a quarter to . . .

twenty to . . .

twenty-five to . . .

. . . -thirty

five after . . .

ten after . . .

a quarter after . . .

twenty after . . .

twenty-five after . . .

Draw the hands.

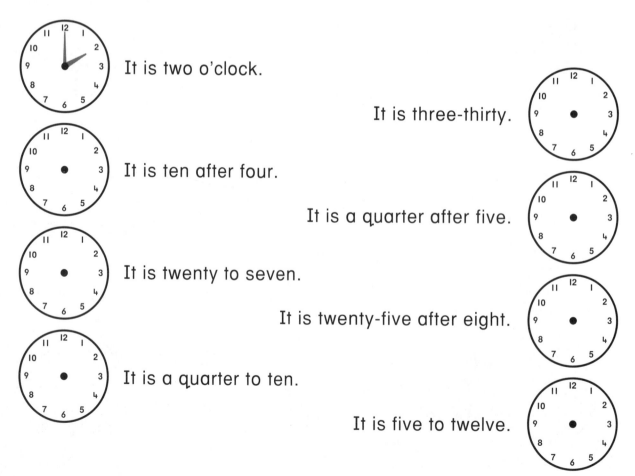

It is two o'clock.

It is ten after four.

It is twenty to seven.

It is a quarter to ten.

It is three-thirty.

It is a quarter after five.

It is twenty-five after eight.

It is five to twelve.

What time is it?

 It is eight o'clock.

It is _____ .

 _____ .

 _____ .

 _____ .

 _____ .

 _____ .

Yesterday

Where were they yesterday?

1. Where was the ball? It was on the teacher's desk.

2. Where was Ann? She _____ behind the blackboard.

3. Where was Mary? She _____ _____ the door.

4. Where were the books? They were on the floor.

5. Where were the flowers? They _____ on the teacher's desk.

6. Where were John and Peter? _____ _____ at their desks.

7. Where was the dog? It _____ near the door.

8. Where were the cats? _____ _____ on the chair.

9. Where was the car? _____ _____ _____ John's desk.

10. Where was the airplane? _____ _____ in the sky.

11. Where were the bottles? _____ _____ _____ Peter's desk.

12. Where was the ruler? _____ _____ _____ the ball.

Write short answers.

1.
Mary

Who was happy yesterday? Mary was.

2.
John

Who was unhappy yesterday? _____ _____.

3.
John and Peter

Who was hot yesterday?
_____ _____ _____ were.

4.
Tom

Who was greedy yesterday? _____ _____.

5.
Mary and Ann

Who was in the car yesterday?
_____ _____ _____ _____.

6. Were you in school yesterday? Yes, I _____.

7. Were you in England yesterday? No, I _____ not.

8. Was it a holiday yesterday? _____.

9. Was it a school day yesterday? _____.

10. Were your friends in school this morning? _____.

11. Were your friends in school last Sunday? _____.

Review

Write questions and answers.

1. sugar

   What was on the table at nine o'clock?
   There was some _____ on the table.

2. a bottle

   What was on the table at six-thirty?
   There was _____ on the table.

3. glasses

   What was _____?
   There were some _____.

4. bread

   What was _____ at a quarter after ten?
   There was _____.

5. a box

   What _____?
   _____.

6. cups

   _____?
   There were _____.

7. water

   _____?
   _____.

8. books

   _____?
   _____.

52

Write questions and answers.

1. Who was in the street at one o'clock?
   There was a boy in the street at one o'clock.

2. Who _____ _____ _____ _____ _____ twenty after one? There _____ no one in the street.

3. Who was in _____ _____ at twenty to two?
   There was a _____.

4. Who _____?
   There was _____.

5. Who _____?
   There _____.

6. Who _____ at twenty-five after two?
   There _____.

7. Who _____?
   _____.

8. _____?
   _____ a police officer _____.

53

Mary   John   Mary and Ann   John and Peter

John   Peter   John and Peter   Mary and Ann

Answer the questions.

1. Did Mary have two apples yesterday?

   Yes, _____ did. She had _____ apples.

2. Did John have four oranges yesterday?

   No, _____ did not. He had three _____.

3. Did Mary and Ann have a basket yesterday?

   Yes, they did. They _____ a _____.

4. Did John and Peter have a boat yesterday?

   No, _____ _____ not. They _____ ___ car.

5. Did John have three books yesterday?

   _____, ____ _____. He _____ _____ _____.

6. Did Peter have four books yesterday?

   _____, he _____. ____ ____ _____ _____.

7. Did John and Peter have a dog yesterday?

   _____, _____ _____. _____ _____ ___ ____.

8. Did Mary and Ann have three cats yesterday?

   _____, _____ _____. _____ _____ _____ _____.

54

Review

Today   **Yesterday**

1.

Today, Mary has a glass of milk for breakfast.
Did she have a glass of milk yesterday?
No, she didn't. She _____ a bowl of soup.

2.

Today, John has a bowl of soup for breakfast.
Did he have a bowl of soup yesterday?
No, ___ _____ . He _____ __ _____ ___
_____ .

3.

Today, Mimi has an apple for lunch.
Did she have an apple for lunch yesterday?
_____ . _____ orange.

4.

Today, Paul has an orange for lunch.
Did he have an orange for lunch yesterday?
_____ . _____ apple.

5.

Today, Peter has a piece of chicken for dinner.
Did he have a piece of chicken yesterday?
_____ . _____
fish.

6.

Today, Ann has a piece of fish for dinner.
Did she have a piece of fish yesterday?
_____ . _____
_____ .

Finish the sentences.

1. Is this a big tree?
Yes, it is. It is very _____.

2. Is this a big tree?
No, it is _____. It is not _____ big.

3. Is this a big ship?
Yes, ___ ___. It ____ ____ ____.

4. Is this a big ship?
_____, ___ ___ ____. It is ___ ____ ____.

5. Is this a dirty shirt?
Yes, ____ ____. It ____ ____ ____.

6. Is this a dirty shirt?
No, ____ ____ ____.
____ ___ __ ____ ____.

7. Is this a good mark?
Yes, ____ ____.
___ ___ ___ ____ ____.

8. Is this a good mark?
_____, ___ ___ ____.
___ ___ __ ____ ____.

56

Answer the questions.

1. Is the boy short?
No, he is not. He is very tall.

2. Is the car new?
No, ____ ____ ____. It ____ very old.

3. Is the ball small?
____, ____ ____ ____. ____ ____ ____
____.

4. Is the doll big?
_____. _____.

5. Is the man rich?
_____. _____ poor.

6. Are the flowers ugly?
___, they _____. _____ beautiful.

7. Is the woman thin?
_____. _____.

8. Is the water cold?
_____. _____ hot.

A. *What can you see on the table?*

1. I can see a bowl of soup.
2. I can see a can of _____.
3. I can see a bottle of _____.
4. I ____ ____ __ glass ___ ____.
5. I ____ ____ __ cup ___ ____.
6. __ ____ ____ __ piece ___ _____.

B. *Look at the picture on the wall and answer the questions.*

1. Can you see a ship? Can you see an airplane?
   I can see a ship but I cannot see ___ _____.
2. Can you see any trees? Can you see any flowers?
   __ ____ ____ some _____ but I _____ ____ any _____.

3. Can you see a man? Can you see a woman?

_____.

4. Can you see a boy? Can you see a girl?

_____.

5. Can you see a dog? Can you see a cat?

_____.

C. *Finish the sentences.*

 1. Can you see a ship in the picture? Yes, I can see it.
 2. Can you see a bottle on the table? Yes, I can see _____.
 3. Can you see some trees in the picture? Yes, I can see _____.
 4. Can you see a girl in the picture? Yes, I can see _____.
 5. Can you see a man in the picture? Yes, I can see _____.
 6. Can you see a dog in the picture? Yes, I can see _____.
 7. Can you see some plates on the table? Yes, I can see _____.
 8. Can you see a can on the table? Yes, I can see _____.

D. *Answer the questions.*

 1. Is the ship big? Yes, it is a _____ ship.
 2. Is the man's hat black? Yes, it is ___ _____ hat.
 3. Are the girl's socks white? Yes, they ____ _____.
 4. Is the dog's tail long? Yes, _____.

E. *Add* **my**, **your**, **its**, **our**, *or* **their**.

1. Where is my ruler? Can you see _____ ruler?

2. Look at that dog. _____ tail is very long.

3. The children are writing in _____ books. They are writing with _____ pens.

4. My father is working now but _____ mother is not working.

5. We are sitting in the classroom and we are listening to _____ teacher.

6. You are careless. _____ work is bad. I am careful. _____ work is good.

7. My shoes are black and your shoes are black. _____ shoes are black.

8. Her shoes are white and his shoes are white. _____ shoes are white.

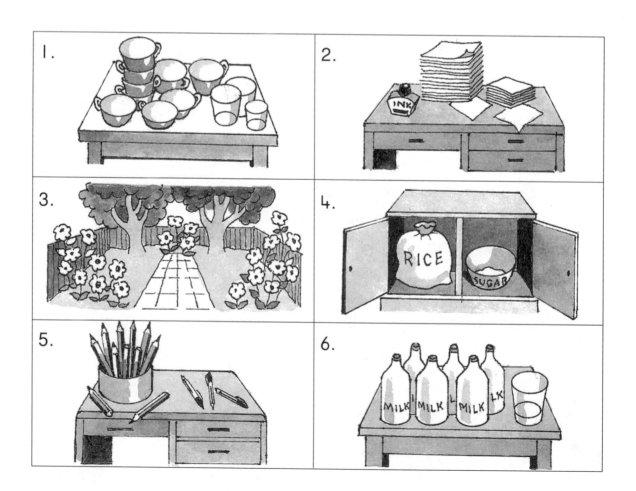

Review

F. *Write questions and answers about the pictures on page 60.*

1. cups? bottles?   Are there any cups? Are there any bottles?
   There are some cups but there aren't any

   _____ .

2. paper? water?   Is there any paper? Is _____?
   There is some _____ but there isn't any

   _____ .

3. flowers? men?   Are _____? _____?
   There _____ .

4. rice? meat?   Is there _____? _____?

   _____ .

5. pencils? paper?   Are _____? Is _____?

   _____ .

6. milk? cookies?   _____? _____?

   _____ .

G. *Write questions and answers about the pictures on page 60.*

1. cups? glasses?   Are there many cups? Are there many
   glasses?
   There are a lot of cups but there aren't many
   glasses.

2. paper? ink?   Is there much paper? Is there much ink?
   There is a lot of _____ but there isn't much

   ____ .

3. flowers? trees?   Are there many flowers? Are _____?

   _____ .

4. rice? sugar?   Is _____? _____?

   _____ .

5. pencils? pens?   _____? _____?

   _____ .

61

Yesterday the children were in a shop.

John   Peter   Paul   Mark   Mary   Ann   Mimi   Rose

H. *Answer the questions.*

1. Who had a very big airplane?   John.

2. Who had a very small airplane?   _____

3. Who had a very big kite?   _____

4. Who had a very small kite?   _____

5. Who had a very thick book?   _____

6. Who had a very thin book?   _____

7. Who had very beautiful dolls?   _____ and

_____

Review

I. *Say what the children had in the shop yesterday.*

1. John had an airplane.
2. Peter _____ an airplane, too.
3. Paul _____ ___ kite.
4. Mark _____ ___ _____ , _____ .
5. Mary _____ .
6. Ann _____ , _____ .
7. Mimi _____ .
8. Rose _____ , _____ .

J. *Answer the questions.*

1. Did John have a small airplane?
   No, he had a very big one.

2. Did Peter have a big airplane?
   No, _____ .

3. Did Paul have a small kite?
   _____ .

4. Did Mark have a big kite?
   _____ .

5. Did Mary have a thin book?
   _____ .

6. Did Ann have a thick book?
   _____ .

7. Did Mimi have an ugly doll?
   _____ .

8. Did Rose have an ugly doll?
   _____ .

Review

Finish the sentences.

1. What time is it? It is _____-thirty. It is time
____ school. John is going ___ school.
He is going to school ____ bus.

2. This desk is made ___ wood.
The can is ____ _____ ___
wood. The pencil ___ _____
___ _____, too.

3. _____ man is a soldier but
_____ man is a sailor.

4. "____ I go outside, please?" "Yes, you ____."
"_____ you."

5. A ruler is longer _____ a pen. A pencil is _____ _____ a ruler.

6. "____ I have a pen, please?" "_____ is a pen." "Thank ____."

7. "Where is the ship? Can you see it?" "Yes, _____ it is!"

8. "Is there anything under your desk?" "No, there isn't ____ under
my desk. There is _____."

9. "Is there anyone outside the room?" "No, there isn't ____ outside
the room. There is _____."

10. "Is there anything in your pocket?" "No, there isn't ____ in my
pocket. There is _____ in my pocket."

11. "Is there ____ in your bag?" "Yes, there is _____ in my bag.
_____ are _____ books in my bag."

12. This year is 19____. Last year _____ 19____. The year before
that _____ 19____.